DISNEY
FROZEN
FEVER
HAIRSTYLES

EDDA USA

DISNEY FROZEN FEVER HAIRSTYLES — Inspired by Anna & Elsa

© 2015 Disney Enterprises, Inc.

Author: Theodora Mjoll Skuladottir Jack
Photographer: Saga Sig, sagasig.com
Stylist: Magnea Einarsdottir
Makeup artist: Karin Kristjana Hindborg
Layout and design: Elsa Nielsen, nielsen.is
Cover design: Gassi.is
Editors: Tinna Proppe, tinna@eddausa.com, Svala Thormodsdottir, svala@edda.is
Printing: Printed in Slovenia

Distributed by Midpoint Book Sales & Distribution

ISBN: 978-1-94078-724-4

www.eddausa.com

ENJOY

... the festive world of **Frozen Fever**. Elsa can't wait to reveal what she's planning for Anna's surprise birthday party, with the help of their good friends Kristoff, Sven, and of course Olaf.

In this book you will find 28 brand new hairdos inspired by the sisters and the **Frozen Fever** short film. The styles vary and are perfect for everything from long, lazy days to festive evenings and special occasions. Each hairstyle is demonstrated with step-by-step photographs and detailed instructions.

Don't hesitate to jump right in and experiment, to combine styles and create your own Frozen Fever-inspired look.

Braidschool

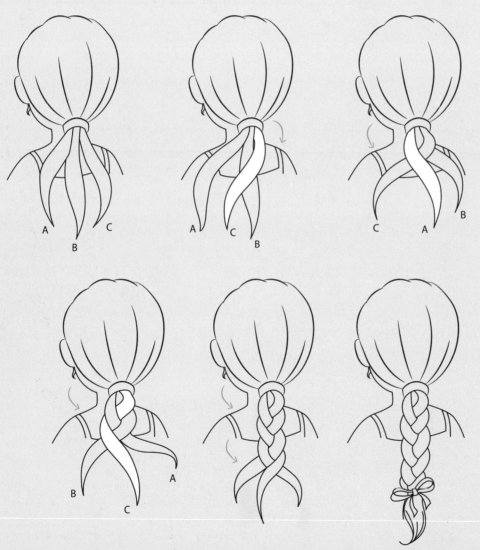

Traditional Braid

- Divide the ponytail into three parts.
- Move the lock of hair on the right over the lock in the middle.
- Now take the lock of hair on the left and move it over the one that is in the middle.
- Move the lock of hair that's now on the right, over the one in the middle.
- Repeat this process until all the ponytail has been braided.

French Braid

- Take three locks of hair along the hairline in the front.
- Move the lock of hair on the right over the lock in the middle.
- Now take the lock of hair on the left and move it over the one that is in the middle.
- Take the lock of hair on the right and add a small lock of hair laying next to it, to the lock.

- Move the lock of hair on the right along with the added hair over the lock of hair in the middle.
- Repeat this process to the lock of hair on the left.
- Repeat this process all the way down or until all the hair on the head has been added to the braid.
- When all the hair has been added to the braid, make a traditional braid down the length of the hair.

Dutch Braid

- Take three locks of hair along the hairline in the front.
- Move the lock of hair on the right under the lock in the middle.
- Now take the lock of hair on the left and move it under the one that is in the middle.
- Take the lock of hair on the right and add a small lock of hair laying next to it, to the lock.

- Move the lock of hair on the right along with the added hair under the lock of hair in the middle.
- Repeat this process to the lock of hair on the left.
- Repeat this process all the way down or until all the hair on the head has been added to the braid.
- When all the hair has been added to the braid, make a traditional braid down the length of the hair.

Rope

- Divide the ponytail in two.
- Twist both locks in the same direction.
- When both locks have been twisted a little bit,
  cross them once in the opposite direction to the twist.
- Keep twisting the locks in the same direction as before
  and cross the locks in the opposite direction to the twist.
- Repeat the process down the length of the hair.

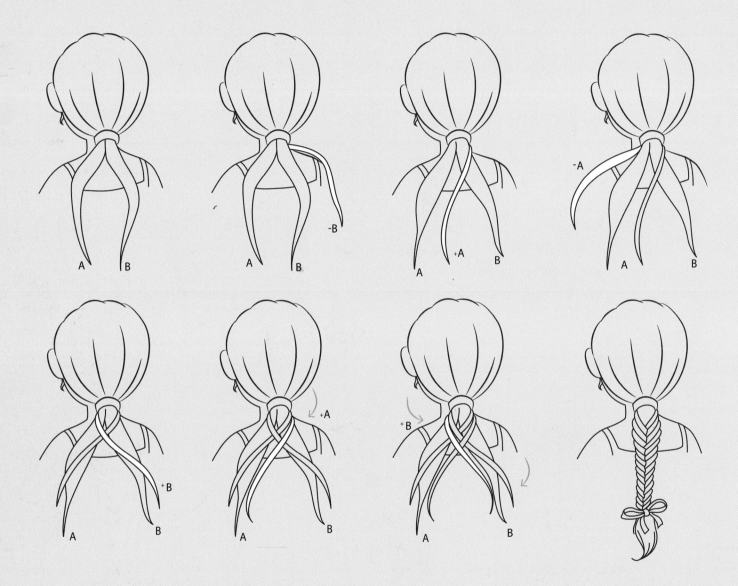

Traditional Fishtail Braid

- Divide the ponytail in two.
- Take a small lock from the outside of the right half of the hair.
- Move the lock over the half of the hair and under the left half of the ponytail.
- Combine the lock with the hair on the left.

- Take an identical lock of hair from the outside of the left half of the hair and move it over to the right part.
- Combine the lock with the hair on the right.
- Repeat this process down the length of the hair.

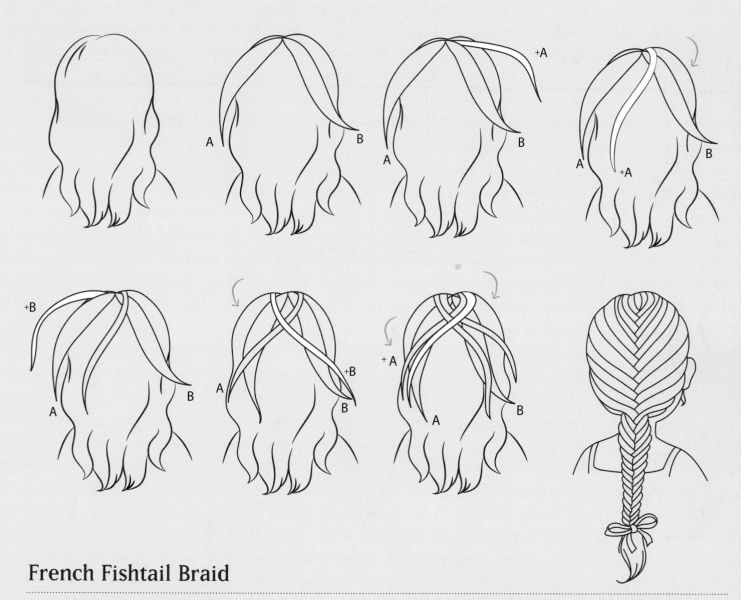

French Fishtail Braid

- Take two locks of hair along the hairline in the front.
- Take a small lock of hair from the head just beside the big lock on the right and move it over the big lock and combine it with the big lock of hair to the left.
- Now take a small lock of hair from the head just beside the big lock of hair on the left and move it over to the lock of hair on the right.

- Take another small lock of hair from the head beside the big lock on the right and move it over the lock of hair on the left.
- Repeat this process down the head until all the hair has been added to the braid.
- When all the hair has been added to the braid, continue by braiding a traditional fishbraid down the length of the hair.

Braided Ladder

1. Take hold of a fairly large lock of hair on top of the head by the forehead.
2. Divide the lock into three strands and braid one round.
3. Take a small lock at the front by the hairline and add it to one strand of the braid.
4. Braid one round.
5. Now take another similar sized lock by the hairline on the other side of the head.
6. Add the lock to one strand of the braid.

Note that this is exactly the same method as for a French braid (see Braidschool), except that only small locks from the hairline are added to the braid, instead of the hair next to the braid, as is done in a normal French braid.

7. Now take a small lock of hair below the first one and add it to the braid, using the same method.
8. Repeat on the other side.
9. Use this method all along the hairline.
10. When you reach below the hairline, use a lock of loose hair the farthest from the hairline, so that the braid will remain loose, maintaining the same texture. Put an elastic band at the end once you have finished braiding.

1.
2.
3.
4.
5.
6.

Ribbon Play

1. Place the hair in a ponytail.
2. Tie a long ribbon around the ponytail. It works well to fasten the ribbon to the elastic band by wrapping it once around it and fastening it with a hairpin. Divide the hair from the ponytail into two pieces.
3. Now make a normal braid, using the ribbon as one strand of the braid (see Braidschool).
4. This is not complicated. Just make sure the ribbon is long enough to braid the length of the ponytail.
5. When all of the hair has been braided, put an elastic band around the end, and tie the ribbon around the elastic band by folding it in two behind the elastic band and tying a knot at the front of the elastic.
6. Make a bow and cut the ribbon to finish.

A Twist of Twists

1. Divide the hair into two sections, horizontally across the back of the head. Secure the top part out of the way.
2. Divide the lower part in two, and make a rope diagonally down the length (see Braidschool), and put a small elastic band at the end.
3. Pull the sides of the rope to make it more irregular and wider.
4. Loosen the top part, and comb the hair to the same side where you made the rope.
5. Make a rope in this section in the same manner as before.
6. Pull the sides of the rope at will, as before.
7. Bring the top rope underneath the lower...
8. ...and over it again. Conceal the end by pressing it into "the bun" which has formed. Pin the top rope securely down by hooking a hairpin in its side and pressing it into the hair.

Summer Braid

1. Clip aside two fairly large locks of hair on either side by the hairline.
2. Make a Dutch braid with all the hair that has not been clipped aside. Make the braid at a slight diagonal.
3. When all of the hair has been added to the braid, pull its strands apart to make it wider.
4. Take the loose lock on one side, and bring it to the back of the head over the braid. Pin it down next to the braid by pressing the hairpin into the braid.
5. Do the same on the other side.
6. Conceal the ends by placing them against the braid and fastening them with a hairpin.
7. You could also take the loose locks on either side and fasten them together with an elastic band, hiding the ends in the braid.

7.

Hidden Tail

1. Place the hair in a ponytail.
2. Take a small lock from the ponytail and wrap it around the elastic band to conceal it. Pin the end down by hooking a hairpin around the end and pushing it in, and under the elastic band. Grasp a small lock of hair on one side of the ponytail.
3. Divide the lock in three sections and braid one round.
4. Now take a small lock of hair from the other side of the ponytail and bring it to the braid.
5. Join the small lock of hair to the strand of the braid closest to it.
6. Braid once.
7. Now take another similar sized lock of hair from beneath the first lock, which you added to the braid, and join it to the strand of the braid closest to it (in the same manner as before).
8. Braid once, and then take another lock of hair from below the former one in the same manner.
9. Repeat the process down the length of the hair. It's best to stand beside the child, pulling the braid close to you while making it.
10. Put a little elastic band at the end of the braid.
11. Hook a hairpin in the top part of the braid, and press the braid towards the head. Fasten the braid against the elastic band by pushing the hairpin into the hair and under the elastic band.

Anna's French Twist

1. Grasp two medium sized locks by the hairline at the front.
2. Cross the locks once over each other.
3. Now take a fairly large lock of hair next to one of the first locks and join them.
4. Do the same on the other side.
5. Cross the locks (including the extra locks) once over one another.
6. Now take two fairly large locks of hair from either side of the crossed locks, and add them in the same manner.
7. Cross the locks over each other like before.
8. Continue this method down the length of the hair.
9. When all the hair has been added to the twist, make an ordinary rope braid down the length of the hair. Then you cross the two locks over one another all the way down.
10. Put an elastic band at the end and fix the twist to your liking.

1.

2.

3.

4.

5.

Braided Double Tail

1. Take all the hair and make a French braid. Start at the front by the forehead, and create the braid directly down the back (see Braidshool).

2. Fasten with an elastic band at the nape of the neck, after all the hair has been added to the braid.

3. Divide the hair from the ponytail into two sections, and braid each part separately. Put an elastic band at both ends.

4. Open the elastic band, and put both ends of the braids through.

5. Fix the ends, so that they face down along the neck.

A Twist and a Ponytail

1. Divide the hair into two sections, across the back of the head. Place an elastic band on the top section by the part.
2. Now divide the lower section into two equal parts, including the ponytail. Clip one side away from the other.
3. Make a rope (see Braidschool) from one half of the ponytail.
4. Bring the rope down along the head, and join the lower part and the rope in a side ponytail.
5. Do the same on the other side.

1.
2.
3.
4.
5.
6.
7.
8.
9.
10.

A Zigzag Twist Braid

1. Divide the hair into four equally large parts, horizontally across the head. The first section goes to the right, the next to the left, then right, and then left. It's best to separate the parts with clips.
2. Loosen the front section.
3. Take two small locks of hair by the part, and cross them, by putting the lock next to the face over the one behind.
4. Take extra hair from either side of the locks, and combine them.

5. Cross the locks of hair with the extra hair once over each other, in the same manner as before. Take more hair and add it in the same way. Repeat this down the section of hair. Note that the smaller the locks you take, the tighter the French twist will be.
6. Now loosen the second section.
7. Go to the other side of the child, and continue making the twist, by adding extra hair to it from the second section, in the same manner as before.

8. Take care not to lose your grip.
9. When you're about to finish the second section, loosen the third section, move to the other side of the child, and continue.
10. When the third section is finished, loosen the last part, and move to the other side of the child. When all the hair has been added to the twist, create an ordinary rope (see Braidschool) down the length of the hair. Place an elastic band at the end. Now you have created a pretty zigzag twist braid.

Loose and Tight

1. Grasp a fairly large lock of hair at the top of the head by the forehead.
2. Divide it into three sections and braid once.
3. Divide one of the outer locks of the braid into two parts.
4. Separate the lock of hair from the braid. Ask the child for help in holding the lock aside.
5. Now divide the lock on the other side into two sections in the same manner.

6. Bring extra locks into the braid, like in an ordinary French braid (see Braidschool) from either side of the braid. Braid once, including the extra locks.
7. Continue this method down the length of the hair, and always put aside half of the locks on the side.
8. When all the hair has been added to the braid, make an ordinary braid down

the length, and secure an elastic band at the end.
9. Grasp the loose locks on either side, and bring them down by the braid.
10. Join all of them with an elastic band underneath the braid at the nape of the neck. Bring the braid to the front, and fix the hair at will.

Over and Under

1. Divide the hair into three sections, vertically down the head, and at a slight diagonal. The middle section is slightly smaller than the other two. Put a small elastic band around the middle section.
2. Separate a small lock from the outside of the right section.
3. Bring the separated lock OVER the right section of hair and under the middle section.
4. Combine the lock with the left section.
5. Now take a small lock from outside of the left section.
6. Bring the separated lock UNDER the left section and over the middle section.
7. Combine the lock with the right section.
8. Now take another small lock furthest from the right, bring it over the hair, under the middle section, and combine it with the left section.
9. Now take a small lock from the left, bring it under the hair, over the middle section, and combine it with the right section.
10. Repeat this method for the length of the hair.
11. Put a small elastic band at the end, when the hair stops reaching into the braid.

1.　2.　3.　4.
5.　6.　7.　8.
9.　10.　11.　12.

A Field of Braids

1. Divide the hair into three sections on a very slight diagonal. Make the middle section bigger than the side sections.
2. Grasp a fairly large lock of hair on top of the head by the forehead.
3. Divide the lock into three sections and braid once. Divide one outer strand of the braid into two parts.
4. Take the lock out of the braid and place aside. Bring an extra lock into the braid, like in an ordinary French braid (see Braidschool).
5. Now divide the lock on the other side into two parts in the same manner.
6. Braid once, including the extra locks.
7. Repeat this method down the middle section, always putting aside half of the locks from the outer strands of the braid, from both sides. When all of the hair has been added to the braid, continue this method down half the ordinary braid. Continue leaving half of the locks from the outer strands aside, until all the way down the ordinary braid.
8. Now take two locks by the hairline at the front, and use the first extra lock that you left behind from the middle braid, as the third part for a new French braid.
9. Braid the three locks together.
10. Now take the second lock you left behind from the middle braid and add it to the new French braid.
11. Repeat this method down the side.
12. Add all of the loose locks from one side of the middle braid to the new braid, and then continue it down the length of the hair. Repeat the whole process on the other side. Fasten the three braids together at the end.

34

An Extremely Thick Braid

1. Place the hair in a ponytail. It works well to use a transparent elastic band.
2. Divide the hair from the ponytail into two sections, separating the front and the back, and put a small elastic band high up in the front section.
3. Open the hair between the elastics, and pull the other half of the ponytail through the hole.
4. Put a small elastic band high up in the section that you pulled through.
5. Open the hair above the elastic band as before.
6. Pull the lower section through in the same manner as before.
7. Place another small elastic band high up in the section, which you pulled through the hole.
8. Repeat this method along the length of the hair.
9. When you have reached the bottom, it works well to join the two sections and pull the hair out to the sides.
10. Fix the hair, and if you would like the braid to be thicker, it works well to pull the outer strands on either side.

Updos and Buns

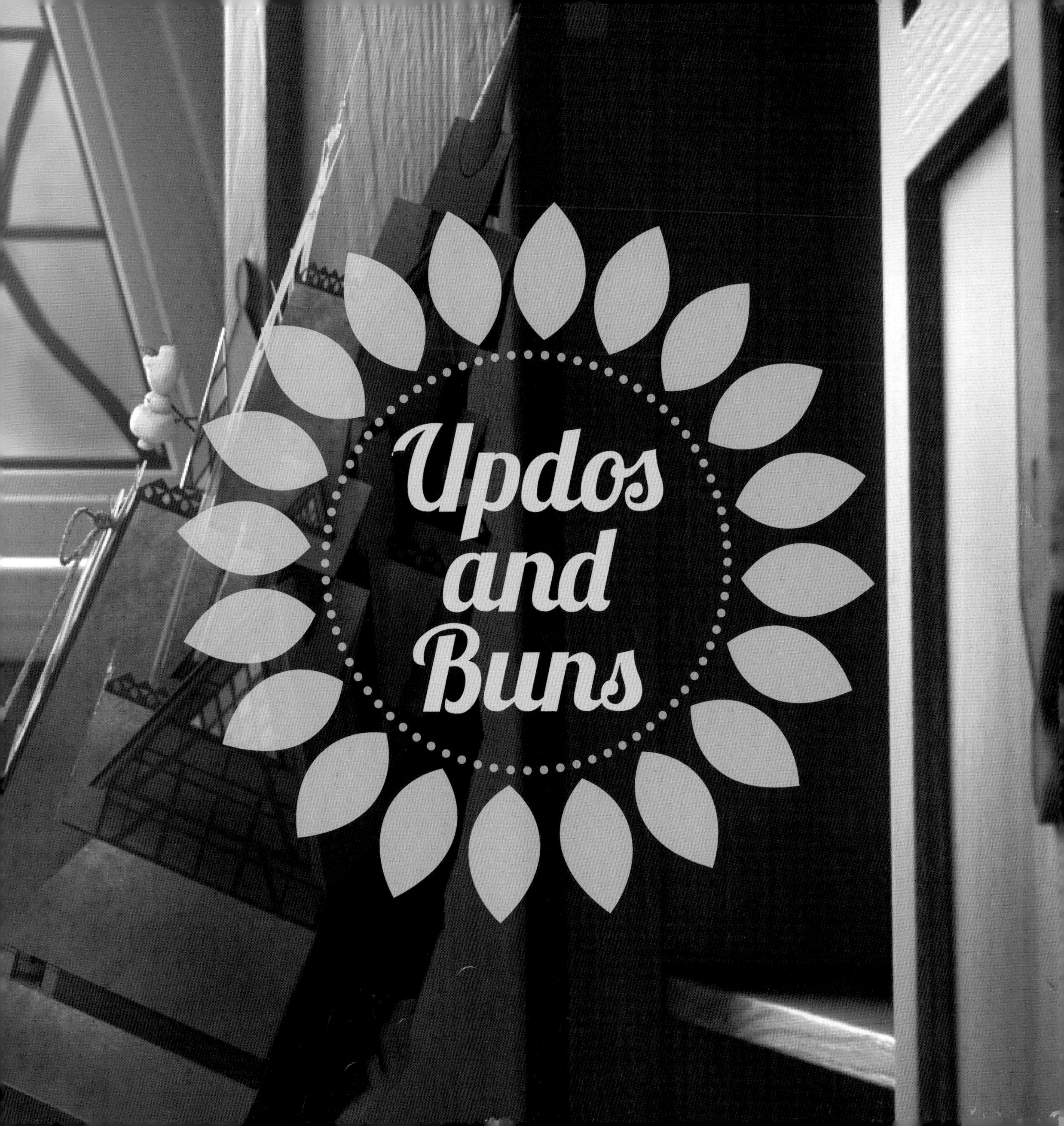

Up, Down, and Around

1. Place the hair in a ponytail.
2. Put a hair donut around the ponytail and grasp a large lock of hair from the ponytail.
3. Braid the lock of hair all the way down and place a small elastic band at the end.
4. Make identical braids from the ponytail.
5. Hold one of the braids with one hand, and the hair donut with the other hand.
6. Wrap the braid tightly around the hair donut by pushing it under and into the middle, over it and under, or until the entire braid has been wrapped around it.
7. Now take another braid and wrap it around the donut in the same manner as before. Start by placing it over the end of the first braid, to hide the elastic band and to make the bun tight.
8. Repeat this, while trying to wrap the braids as tightly as possible.
9. At the end, it can be quite tricky to wrap the braid around the donut. Do not give up and don't be afraid to pull the hairdo in all directions.
10. When all the braids have been added to the bun, you can fix it at will. Bring the braids closer together if necessary and fasten them with a few hairpins, if you wish.

A Side Bun

1. Make a side part in the hair at the front. Grasp a large lock of hair by the part on the side, closest to the ear.
2. Divide the lock into three sections and start making a French braid along the back (see Braidschool).
3. Add large locks of hair to the braid, and keep it loose.
4. Braid along the hairline.
5. When you reach the other side, it's best to face the child to braid the hair toward yourself.
6. Braid the hair loosely over the ear and toward the face. When all the hair has been added to the braid, make an ordinary braid for the length of the hair and place it in an elastic band.
7. Pull and fix the strands of the braid.
8. Fold in the end to conceal it.
9. Make a flat bun from the braid, by bringing it back to the ear, and placing it flatly in a circle.
10. Hold it tightly with one hand while pinning the bun down. It's best to hook a hairpin in the outer strands of the braid, pressing the pin in the hair.

Bulging Ponytail

1. Divide the hair into two sections, horizontally across the back of the head, and put the top section into a ponytail.
2. Bring the hair from the ponytail over toward the forehead.
3. Use two hairpins for both sides of the ponytail. Pin the sides so that the ends of the hairpins stick together.
4. Now bring the hair from the ponytail toward the back of the head.
5. Put a little elastic band around the ponytail.
6. Roll the ends of the hair up and place them under the hair bulge which has formed.
7. Pin the hair down to the small elastic band, by hooking a hairpin into both the elastic band and the root of the hair, pressing the hairpin into the bulge and under the ponytail.
8. Push the ends underneath the bulge, and pin it down in the same manner, until the hairdo stays in place.

1.
2.
3.
4.
5.
6.
7.
8.
9.
10.

Spring Bun

1. Divide the hair into two sections, across the back of the head, and place the hair in a low ponytail. Make a side part in the top section, and let the hair lie on either side of the head.
2. Put a hair donut around the ponytail and fasten it down with a hairpin, by hooking it into both the donut and the root of the hair, pressing the hairpin into the hair towards the elastic band. It's best to do this in 3-4 places.
3. Lay the hair evenly over the donut, and put a tight elastic band around it to form a pretty bun.
4. Take the loose hair from one side and twist it, bringing it to the back of the head. It works best to pull the sides of the twist with one hand, to make it bigger and more textured.
5. Bring the twist back along the head and over the bun. Pin it down against the bun, by sticking the hairpin around the twist and into the bun.
6. Do the same on the other side.
7. Take the twist and add the hair, that was left over from the bun, into the twist.
8. Twist the hair tightly.
9. Bring the twist underneath the bun and add the rest of the hair to it in the same way.
10. Fasten the end of the twist against the bun.

Braided Circle

1. Place hair in a ponytail.
2. Make several small braids from the ponytail, securing the end of each with an elastic band.
3. Pull the outer strands of the braids to add texture.
4. Lay one of the braids flat in a circle against the hair, a couple of inches above the elastic band, and pin it down.
5. Take another braid, and lay it in the same manner against the hair, below the first braid, and pin it down.
6. Repeat this, until all the braids have been fastened above the elastic band. Now take the ends of the braids, continue placing them in a circle, and fasten them in the same manner.
7. It's best to conceal the ends of the braids by pressing them into and under the braids. Pin the braids securely down to form a pretty braided bun.

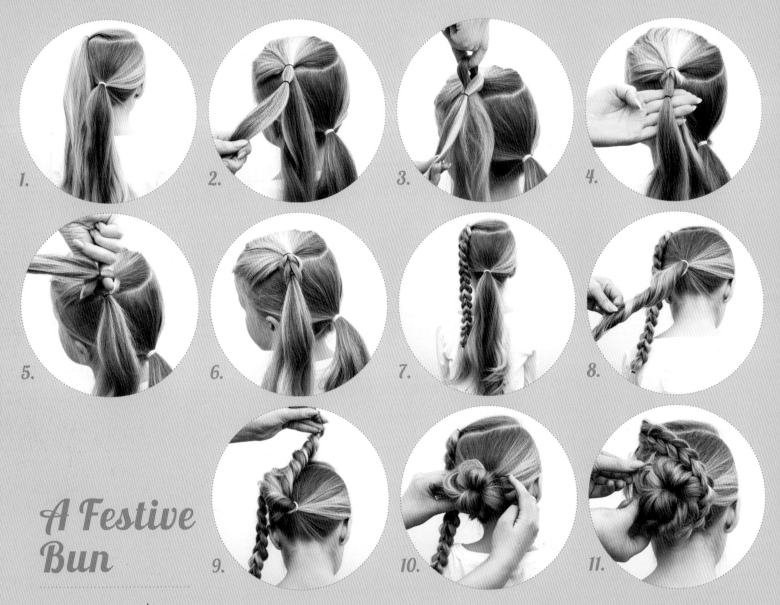

A Festive Bun

1. Take a large section of hair on top of the head and place in a ponytail. Take the rest of the hair and place in another ponytail.
2. Divide the hair from the top ponytail into two sections, separating the front and the back, and put a small elastic band high in the top section.
3. Open the hair between the elastic bands, and pull the lower part of the ponytail through the hole.
4. Place a small elastic band high in the section that you just pulled through.
5. Open the hair above the elastic band as before.
6. Pull the bottom section through in the same manner as before, and secure another small elastic band in the section that which you just pulled through the hole.
7. Repeat this method for the length of the hair.
8. Moving on to the second ponytail, twist the entire ponytail and gently pull on the sides of the twist to add texture and fullness.
9. Lay the twist loosely around the ponytail to form a bun.
10. Pin the bun down by sticking hairpins in the strands farthest from the roots of the hair, and pressing the hairpin in toward the elastic band.
11. Lay the braid around the bun, and pin it in a few places against the bun.

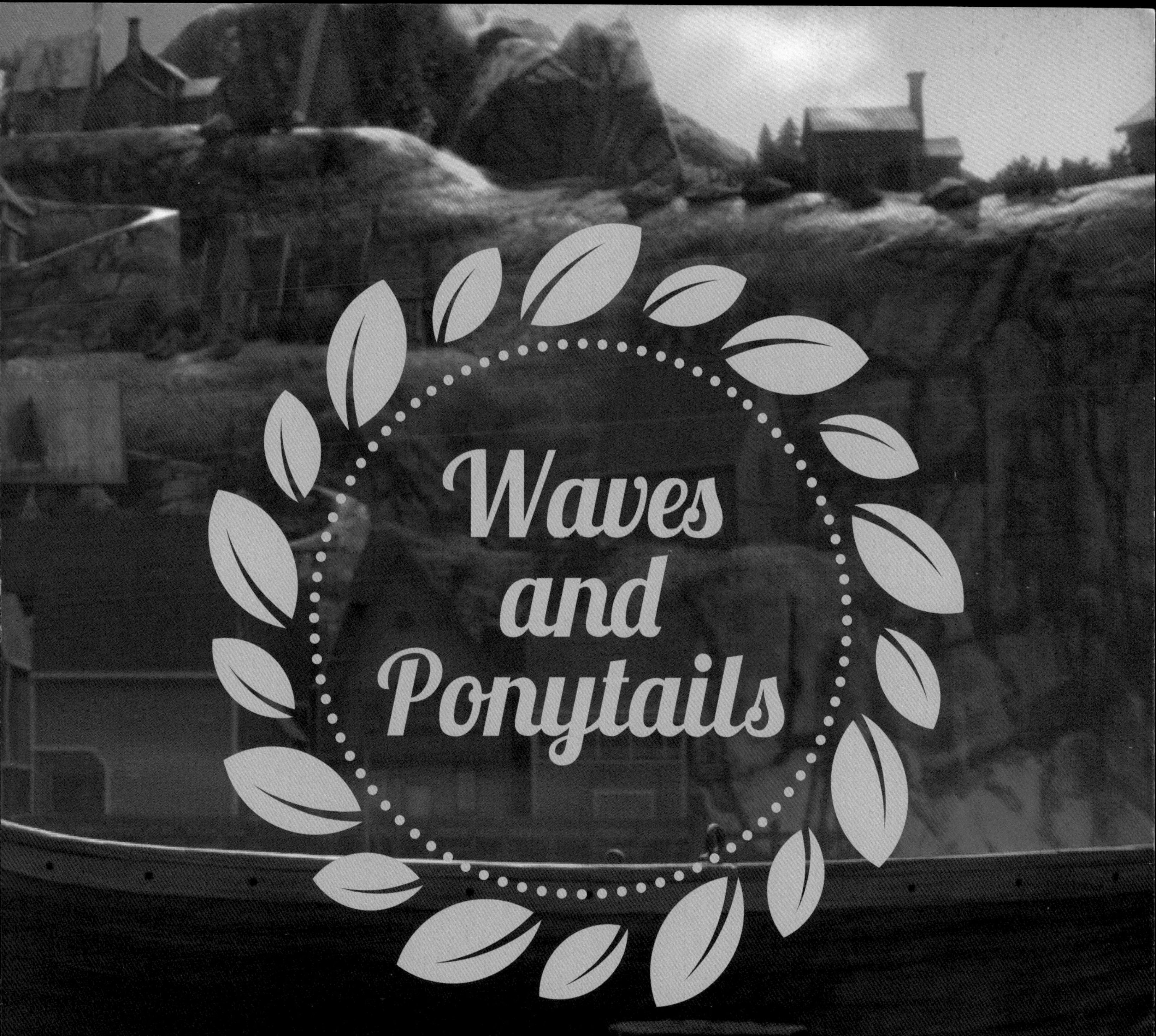
Waves
and
Ponytails

1.

2.

4.

3.

Four into One

1. Make a side part in the hair at the front. Take a medium sized lock of hair from the dominant side.
2. Braid the lock and put an elastic band at the end.
3. Take another similar sized lock of hair below the first one, and braid similarly. Fasten the braids together at the end with an elastic band.

4. On the other side, make two braids, one below the other, and fasten all four braids together.

NOTE: This hairstyle works well for girls who are growing their bangs out, or for those who would like to get their bangs/hair off their face.

A Flow of Locks

1. Take two small locks of hair from either side of the head, from the hairline by the ears. Bring the two locks to the back of the head.
2. Join the locks with a small elastic band.
3. Take hold of similar sized locks from the hairline, just below the first ones, and bring them to the back of the head.
4. Join the locks with a small elastic band, directly below the first elastic. It works well to place the elastics on a slight diagonal.
5. Take two more locks of hair below the original ones and repeat the process.
6. Repeat this down the length of the hair as you please, as long as it suits the hair.

1.
2.
3.
4.
5.
6.

The Princess Fishtail Braid

1. Make a center part in the hair at the front. Grasp a large lock by the part on one side.
2. Make a fishtail braid (see Braidschool) in this part. It is best to stand behind the child, braiding toward the back.
3. Don't make the braid too long. Put an elastic band at the end and pull the strands of the braid if you wish to make it wider and more irregular.
4. Make an identical braid on the other side, and join them at the back of the head with a small elastic band.
5. Take a small lock from the ponytail and wrap it around the elastic band.
6. Fasten the end with another small elastic band. It works well to push the wrapped hair slightly over the elastic band to hide it.

1.
2.
3.
4.
5.
6.
7.
8.
9.
10.
11.

Braided
Wreath

1. Grasp a large lock of hair by the part on one side.
2. Divide the lock into three sections, and braid one round toward the back of the head.
3. Bring a large lock of hair from the top of the head down to the braid, and add it to it. Braid once.
4. Now take a very small lock of hair from beneath the braid and add it.
5. This braid is made exactly like a French braid (see Braidschool), except that from above you add large locks, and from below you add small locks.
6. Repeat this method horizontally around the head.
7. When you reach the other side, it works well to move in front of the child to braid to the front of the head.
8. Bring the braid toward the forehead in the same manner.
9. When all the hair from the top has been added to the braid, make an ordinary braid.
10. Pull the strands of the braid at will.
11. Bring the end of the braid to the French braid, forming a braided circle. Fasten the braids together with a hairpin. It works well to stick the hairpin into the end of the braid, pushing it against the hair.

1.

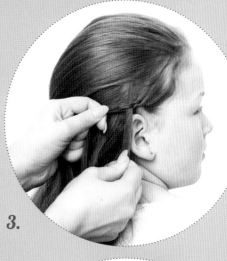

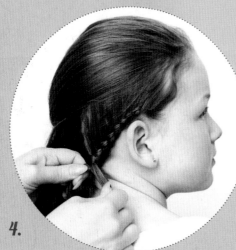

2.

3.

4.

5.

6.

Braids and Curls

1. Divide the hair into two sections, diagonally across the head, and put the top section in a side ponytail by the hairline.
2. Take a small lock of hair from the bottom section, at the front by the face.
3. Make a Dutch braid (see Braidschool) along the hairline, adding the smallest locks possible to the braid.
4. Keep the braid as close to the hairline as you can.
5. When the entire bottom section has been added to the Dutch braid, make an ordinary braid down the length of the hair, and put a small elastic band at the end.
6. Wrap the braid tightly once around the elastic band and conceal the end behind the braid.
7. Hold the braid tightly and pin it down by the elastic band, by hooking a hairpin in the outermost strand of the braid, and pressing it down into and under the elastic band.

7.

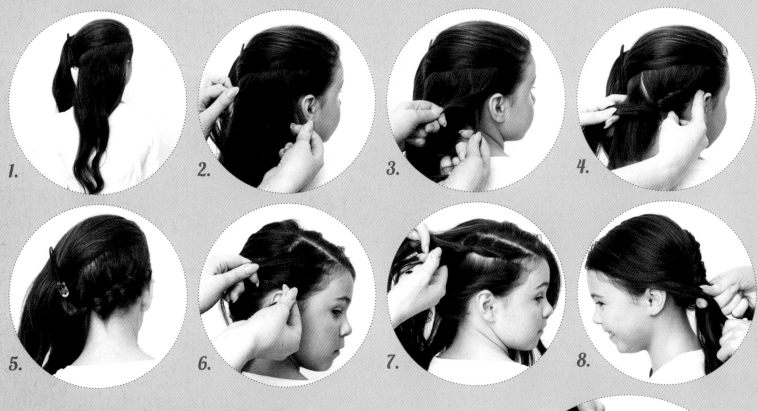

1.
2.
3.
4.
5.
6.
7.
8.

A Twist of Flowers

1. Divide the hair into two sections, diagonally across the head. Clip the top section away.
2. Take two small locks of hair by the hairline from the bottom section, and cross them over each other.
3. Take extra hair from either side of the two locks and join them.
4. Cross the locks, with the extra hair, once.
5. Repeat this method down along the hairline, or until the whole bottom section has been added to the twist. Put an elastic band in the hair by the hairline.
6. Loosen the top section of hair, grasp two locks by the hairline at the front, and cross them once over each other.
7. Make a French twist in the top section in the same manner as you did for the bottom section.
8. Make the twist as close to the part as you can.
9. When the whole top section has been added to the twist, bring it toward the bottom section, and put an elastic band around both parts. Adjust the twist at will.

9.

A Triple Topsytail

1. Divide the hair into three sections diagonally down the head, and place an elastic band around each part separately by the hairline.
2. The division should create a pretty side part at the front hairline.
3. Open the hair behind the elastic band with your fingers.
4. Push the whole ponytail through the hole.
5. A twist will form behind the elastic band.
6. Tighten the ponytail firmly, by pulling the hair below the elastic band in opposite directions.
7. Repeat this process for the other two ponytails.
8. Combine the hair from the three ponytails. This is also suitable for curly hair.

1.

2.

3.

4.

5.

Elsa's Birthday Braid

1. Grasp a large section of the hair on top of the head, and clip the rest away.
2. Make a fishtail braid in this section along the length of the hair.
3. Create a side ponytail from the lower section. Bring the fishtail braid to the ponytail and make a hole in the braid where it reaches the ponytail. Pull the ponytail through the braid.
4. Adjust the braid. Make the braid bigger by pulling the sides in opposite directions.
5. Fasten the braid to the ponytail, by sticking a hairpin into the braid by the elastic band, and pushing it into and under the ponytail.

Checkered Braid

1. Divide the hair into two sections, horizontally across the back of the head, and put the top part in an elastic band.
2. Take a small lock from the ponytail and wrap it around the elastic band to conceal it. Fasten the end of the lock by the elastic band with a hairpin.
3. Divide the ponytail into four equal parts.

4. Now take part 4 aside (the furthest away).
5. Bring part 4 over part 3.
6. Now bring part 4 under part 2.
7. Bring part 4 over part 1 and then under part 1.
8. Bring part 4 over part 2 and under part 3.
9. Now bring part 4 over part 3, and continue.
10. Continue this until part 4 has become too short to continue. Then place the hair in an elastic band.

11. Take a small strand from the ponytail and wrap it around the elastic band. After three rounds, bring the lock behind the braid and join the end with a small lock from the ponytail. Fasten them together with an elastic band.

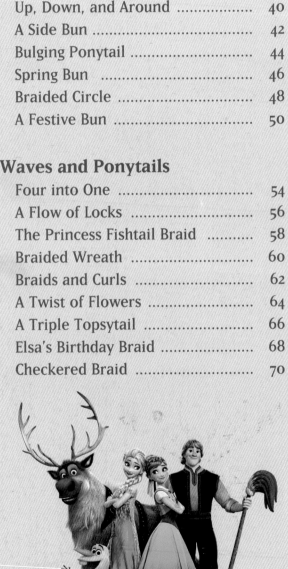